The Spiral of the Seasons

Books by John G. Sullivan

To Come to Life More Fully:
An East West Journey
(1990)

Living Large:
Transformative Work at the Intersection
of Ethics and Spirituality
(2004)

The Spiral of the Seasons

Welcoming the Gifts of Later Life

John G. Sullivan, PhD

Manufactured in the United States of America.

Second Journey Publications
4 Wellesley Place
Chapel Hill, NC 27517
(919) 403-0432
www.SecondJourney.org

ISBN 978-0-615-31305-4

Partial underwriting for the publication of this book was provided by the Mary Duke Biddle Foundation.

Design by Michael Brady Design

Photo credits: Front cover by Yacop; pp. vii–viii, Christian Kitazume; p. 8, Ben Hodgson; pp. 21–22, Lanzi H. Hoffmeister; pp. 41–42, John Nyberg; p. 60, Estormiz; p. 74, Horton Group.

Acknowledgments

I thank my wife, Gregg, whose presence enriches my work and my life. She is my love.

I thank my family over generations: grandparents, parents, children, grandchildren. I realize each day that we do indeed stand in the midst of seven generations. In all we do, may we honor the ancestors, companion our contemporaries, and serve the children.

I thank my colleagues at Second Journey, especially Bolton and Lisa Anthony who, together with graphic designer Michael Brady, saw this work into form. The book is better because of their loving care.

I thank my teaching colleagues at Tai Sophia Institute in Laurel, Maryland, especially Robert Duggan, Dianne Connelly, Anne Baker, and Helen Mitchell. They continue to shape my thinking and teaching.

I thank my colleagues at Elon University who, over decades, have supported and enhanced my work, especially the members of the Elon Philosophy Department.

I thank those who have been teachers and elders to me, especially Frederick and Claske Franck, Maynard Adams, and, in the spirit, Thich Nhat Hanh and Archbishop Desmond Tutu.

I come with deep respect to the wider natural world, the Great Family of all creatures, and the Great Mystery that surrounds us. In and towards this communion, I experience gratefulness and great fullness.

I thank all those — known and unknown, named and unnamed — whose loving-kindness, compassion, sympathetic joy, and equanimity have touched me deeply.

As W. B. Yeats says in his poem "Gratitude to the Unknown Instructors":

> What they undertook to do
> they brought to pass;
> All things hung like a drop of dew
> upon a blade of grass.

Introduction

Once upon a time, a young prince learned of a pearl of great price — a pearl that would bring all good things. He wandered far and wide — through kingdoms and cities, across mountains and seas. Many had heard of the jewel; no one could say where it could be found. After seeking for many years, the prince returned home, exhausted and disappointed. Before entering the palace of his father and mother, he stopped in the courtyard to wash away the dust of his journeys. As he gazed into the mirror-like water, he caught sight of the pearl. The pearl he sought shone forth from his forehead.

Was the pearl there all along? Did the seeking serve to make it manifest? Was it only evident after the striving ceased and the prince returned — returned to himself, to his place, to elemental realities such as the water in the crystal-clear pool?

This story with its paradoxical qualities is an overture to this book. We are seeking a vibrant spirituality for later life. Like seeking the pearl, this quest seems elusive. How are we to find a path with a heart — especially in later life? Perhaps by following our heart, by following what is truly beautiful.

The wise ones of old understood that the *true*, the *good*, and the *beautiful* were three facets of one reality. Three doors to enter and live life more fully. What is real attracts us under the aspects of what we see as good, what we respond to as beautiful. Here is where we begin.

In this set of essays, we shall follow the beautiful as manifested in the four seasons, as understood by the sages of ancient China and Japan. And we shall also follow the beautiful as presented in the four stages of life as understood by the sages of ancient India:

> In Spring, we are in the stage of Student.
>
> In Summer, we move to the stage of Householder.
>
> In Autumn, we enter the stage of Forest Dweller.
>
> In Winter, we drop into the world of the Sage.

In overlaying the four stages of life on the four seasons, we have a simple framework with immense power, represented by the diagram on the facing page. In graphic form, we have the following: Notice that there is an arc of ascent — from Spring to Summer, or, alternately, from Student to Householder. And there is an arc of descent — from Autumn to Winter, or, alternately, from Forest Dweller to Sage.

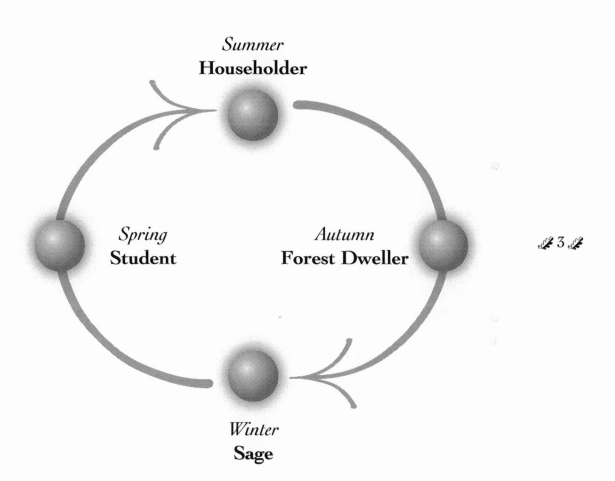

Summer
Householder

Spring
Student

Autumn
Forest Dweller

Winter
Sage

3

In other cultures and other times, these two turning points were marked with separate initiations. The first initiation is the passage from *Student* to *Householder*. This initiation normally took place when the young were ready to enter the wider world of work (contributing to the community in useful ways) and the deeper world of love (typically marrying and beginning a family of their own). This upward and outward initiation into adulthood has been called an Initiation of Fire. We feel it as we move in imagination from the early growth of Spring to the full power of the sun in Summer. This passage taught the initiates how to operate in the wider world of love and work and how to take responsibility for units larger than themselves.

The second initiation typically happened when the children left home and the task of child rearing was complete. We might think of such a shift occurring at retirement where we acknowledge both the completion of child rearing and the end of one's structured work life. The second transition is from *Householder* to *Forest Dweller* and *Sage*. In shorthand, this is an initiation into elderhood. This downward and inward transition into elderhood has been called the Night Sea Journey. The name becomes clearer when we notice that in many cultures the winter is associated with the deep waters.

While the first initiation has a flavor of the sun at midday, the second initiation has the flavor of the moon over the waters at midnight.

Our culture is very much at home in the first half of life. We are at home in doing, in striving, in achieving. The quest is toward fame and fortune. We still have weak remnants of the Student-to-Householder initiation, though usually offered long before a man or woman is truly an adult in the culture's eyes. There are hardly any remnants remaining of the second initiation — into the stage of elder. This initiation is in the downward and inward energy of Autumn and Winter. It involves simplifying and returning to a fuller relationship to the natural world. It involves releasing into a place where there is less doing or achieving and, paradoxically, more ability to be more present to life. Learning to dwell in the depth of life allows one to participate in deeper currents than one's own energy alone. Here the elder takes instruction from Autumn and Winter. How to be with the downward energy without labeling it decline. How to see, in waterfall energy, new possibilities to age consciously and joyously and with wholly new capacities to be in life differently.[1] Turning with the seasons. Returning to what is central to life.

This book is directed primarily to those seeking to live differently in the elder phase of life, that is to say, after retirement. I turned to

the lessons of the arc of descent when I myself retired at age 70, after teaching for 36 years at Elon University in North Carolina. Even before retirement, I began to explore what I took to be tasks of an elder:

- ❧ To keep the little things little and the big things big
- ❧ To encourage creativity (in oneself and others)
- ❧ To bless the young[2]

This book promises a way to tap the Autumn and Winter energies — energies of release, of letting go and letting be, of coming home to what truly matters. Rising energy looks to time and steps. Yet it need not be filled with stressful striving. Falling energy looks to releasing from those thoughts and emotions that prevent us from seeing that we already have all we seek. Paradoxically, the pearl of great price is already in us. Embedded in our foreheads. While we strive, we do not see our own beauty, our own deep nature. However, others may see us as we are — in our surface struggles and in our deep and unrepeatable beauty. Imagine seeing ourselves and all given to our care as full beings — imperfect, in progress and yet already home. If, in later life, we can learn such lessons of Forest Dweller and Sage, how much

more satisfying will we find our miraculous life. When the beautiful
falling energy of Autumn and Winter is not seen as "less than"
the beautiful rising energy of Spring and Summer, we are in a
position to value all phases of life. Then rising energy need not be a
recipe for burnout, and falling energy need not be seen as decline.
Knowing this, we can resonate with the poet Wun-Men:

> Ten thousand flowers in spring,
> The moon in autumn,
> A cool breeze in summer,
> Snow in winter.
> If your mind isn't clouded by unnecessary things,
> This is the best season of your life.[3]

Chapter 1

Spring's Stirrings: The Art of Being a Beginner

In spring we are all children again. We experience beginnings — life on the move, arising before our eyes. Everything new. Everything now. "Now the ears of my ears awake and now the eyes of my eyes are opened."[1]

My teaching colleagues suggest that when we are tempted to say: *"It's difficult — I can't,"* we might shift to saying, *"I am a beginner at this. I can seek help. I can learn."*[2] This is compassionate counsel. We are all beginners in many arenas. The invitation is to help one another.

Beginners in many arenas. Apprentices — with some skill — in others. Masters and virtuosos rarely.[3] In the Spring, we think of new growth and the awe and joy of beginnings.

Zen practitioners give us an even deeper perspective by celebrating "beginner's mind" throughout all the circumstances of our lives. Zen master, Shunryu Suzuki tells us:

> In Japan we have the phrase *shoshin*, which means "beginner's mind." The goal of practice is always to keep our beginner's mind . . . Our "original mind" includes everything within itself. It is always rich and sufficient within itself. . . . If your mind is empty, it is always ready for anything; it is open to everything. In the beginner's mind there are many possibilities; in the expert's mind there are few.[4]

Consider the season of Spring and the notion of "beginner's mind." Can we carry this touch of Spring into all the seasons of a year or a life? Ancient Chinese healers said "yes." They taught that all of the seasons were present in any of the seasons. To be sure, the note of Spring is sounded most strongly in the season of Spring. However, with practice, we can hear the note of springtime beginnings in Summer and Autumn and Winter too. The art of being a beginner is evident when we are at the stage of youthful student. (And we remain students lifelong.) The art of being a beginner has a different flavor when we cultivate it in the Summer of our Householder years. And, as we enter the later years of life — the Autumn and Winter stages — surely we are a beginner at doing this phase of life too. In short, there is a permanent place for being a beginner wherever we are in our life.

Constant Beginnings

In a sense, we are always beginning again. We get good at kindergarten and then we move to first grade. Just when we are getting the hang of elementary school, we move to middle school and then high school. We learn how to operate in high school and, in a flash, we begin again in college. After our school years, we start anew in the work world. We are novices, rookies, still wet behind the ears. Perhaps we marry and have barely adjusted to marriage when we begin again with children. And so it goes. When we move into mature competence at our work and a settled feeling of seeing the children into adulthood, retirement arrives. And we begin again, seeking out what it means to be an elder, what it means to simplify and enter the deep waters. How do we preserve beginner's mind, in the best sense, throughout the seasons of a life?

Here is a nursery rhyme:

> There was an old man named Michael Finnegan
> He had whiskers on his chin again
> Cut them off and they grew in again
> Poor old Michael Finnegan . . . . Begin again.

There was an old man named Michael Finnegan

He kicked up an awful dinnegann

Because they said he must not sing again

Poor old Michael Finnegan . . . . Begin again.

There is likewise a comic Irish ballad called "Finnegan's Wake." In the song, Tim Finnegan dies. His body is laid out at his house for an Irish wake, complete with the expected food and drink. As the evening progresses, the wake turns into a brawl, "woman to woman and man to man." A noggin of whiskey goes flying and spills on the corpse. Tim Finnegan awakes! A "wake" and "awake." Round and round. We are all Finnegan and we constantly "Begin again."

Beginning Again after a Fall

"Time for you to get back up," my father said. I was young, riding horseback, and had taken a serious spill. After checking to make sure the damage was not dire, my father made sure I got back on the horse. "Time to get up and continue," he said.

Beginning again after a fall. Sometimes, the fall is something out of our control. A setback, a natural disaster, a disappointment, a betrayal, an injustice suffered. Sometimes the fall is our doing. We caused the suffering to others and to ourselves and to the web of relationships that surround us. Furthermore, our harsh words or deeds hardened the hearts of those affected.[5] What is needed is a reversal — *metanoia*, in the Greek — a change of direction.

Here, beginning again means to "true ourselves up," to remember and return to who we are at our depth, to heed the call of our larger and deeper self. The Roman Catholic tradition advised three steps and called them (1) confession, (2) contrition, and (3) satisfaction. We can think of them as mirroring three aspects of the present moment — the past-in-the-present, the present-in-the-present, and the future-in-the-present.

We find these three steps embedded in the Twelve-Step Program of Alcoholics Anonymous. Much earlier, we find them expressed poetically in Dante's *Divine Comedy*. Dante places the three steps at the doorway to inner work.[6] In Dante's imagery, the first step is white marble, polished like a mirror. The second step is rough, black and broken, the color of grief. The third step is blood-red porphyry, representing sacrifices needed to put things right. Here is how we might think of them:

- *Confession*: The marble mirror asks us to admit what we have done — to say it out loud, preferably to another human being, to own the action that caused harm — whether an act of commission or omission.
- *Contrition*: The black step invites us to bring our heart into the picture. To feel and express sorrow for the suffering caused — to others and ourself and the web of trust that sustains us. This step also prompts us to ask for forgiveness from those we have wronged, where that is appropriate.
- *Satisfaction*: The blood-red porphyry step asks us to amend our ways, to redirect our conduct, to repair so far as possible the harm we have caused. We are called to seek a future path more consonant with our own deep nature and the nature of our life together. We are asked to finish the "turn around" by restoring harmony, outwardly repairing the harm, and inwardly committing ourselves to install the practices and gather the support to proceed in healthier fashion (satis-facere = to make it enough).

This older way of beginning again after a fall is down-to-earth, honest and robust, much like tough love. We are called to face, in sorrow, what is unresolved in us, to dismantle destructive habits and to walk a more positive path. The practice of the three steps is not meant to have us dwell in guilt or regret. In fact, such regression often is a kind of "sentimentality in disguise." Instead the three steps point us to the inner work of practice whereby we stop, look, and listen to what is ours to do. The restorative work is done with compassionate gaze, with help at hand — remembering that we are not solitary beings but already and always enfolded in communal bonds. Where we were unskilled, we can develop skills. Where we were mindless, we can practice mindfulness. Where we were unloving, we can enkindle loving-kindness.

The mystic Rumi encourages us:

> Come, come, whoever you are.
> Wanderer, worshipper, lover of leaving.
> It doesn't matter.
> Ours is not a caravan of despair.
> Come, even if you have broken your vow a thousand times,
> Come, yet again, come, come.[7]

Steady As We Go — Celebrating the Good and the Beautiful

    To reduce unnecessary suffering and to promote creative possibility for our common life — this is a worthy mission. The three steps, like three notes on a xylophone, aid us to reverse patterns that diminish life. Yet there is another side — to affirm and celebrate the good and the beautiful. This is also a part of a daily "beginning again."

How do you keep the music playing?
How do you make it last?
How do you keep the song from fading too fast?
How do you lose yourself in someone
And never lose your way?
How do you not run out of new things to say?

And since we know we're always changing
How can it be the same?
And tell me how year after year
You're sure your heart will fall apart
Each time you hear his name?
I know the way I feel for you is now or never.

The more I love the more I am afraid
that in your eyes I may not see forever —
Forever.

If we can be the best of lovers yet be the best of friends,
If we can try with every day to make it better as it grows
With any luck, then I suppose
The music never ends.[8]

Suppose we distinguish between *phenomena* and the *stories we tell about the phenomena*.[9] Then we can ask: When I go home today, do I see my spouse or parent as *phenomena-ever-able-to-surprise-me*, or do I see that spouse or parent as covered over with stories so I do not have to see anew and listen anew and respect anew and love anew? When I go to the place where I work or volunteer, do I see my co-workers as *phenomena-ever-able-to-surprise-me* or do I see them as storied over? How do we keep the music playing? How do we make it last? Is not each day a great gift of beginning anew, always anew?

A Chinese saying instructs: "Renew yourself completely each day; do it again and again and forever again." I would amplify by adding: "Renew your relationships completely each day; do it again and again and forever again."

Dwelling Always at the Beginning

"As it was in the beginning, is now and ever shall be. Amen."
At our core, we are linked to the revolving universe and the Ever-
present Origin — the still point of the turning world, the love that
moves the sun and the other stars.[10] In the eternal present, before
creation, so teaches Islam, we — the human ones — said "Yes" to
God.[11] We agreed, in a time before time, to serve in what we might
call the Great Work and the Great Love. Such primal directedness
is inscribed in our very being. In the biblical account, we are
created in the image and likeness of God.[12] To dwell always at the
beginning is to engage in remembrance of ourselves in relationship
to the Great Mystery, the ground and goal of our being and
becoming.

At the deepest level, we stand at this point — in time and out of
time. Foolish beings of wayward passions[13] yet touched, through
and through, by the divine. To see one another in this way is to
love with exquisite courtesy. As if the play were ending and we let
go of our roles to take a bow. Brothers and sisters of royal lineage.
Realizing that we are and are not the roles we play.

Forever Young

We live in a youth culture. When youth is the measuring stick, then, as we age, all seems to be decline. Perhaps we have confused youth with vitality. To be vital, interested, engaged in ongoing learning and consistent renewal — perhaps this says it better. Earlier I spoke about how there was a touch of Spring in every stage of life — Student and Householder, Forest Dweller and Sage. A unique vitality for each task. If so, we can reclaim the words about youth, without having to cancel the gift of years and without having to pretend we are what we are not. I invite you to be blessed by listening to the Bob Dylan song "Forever Young" with new ears:

> May God bless and keep you always,
> May your wishes all come true,
> May you always do for others
> And let others do for you.
> May you build a ladder to the stars
> And climb on every rung,
> May you stay forever young,
> Forever young, forever young,
> May you stay forever young.

May you grow up to be righteous,
May you grow up to be true,
May you always know the truth
And see the lights surrounding you.
May you always be courageous,
Stand upright and be strong,
May you stay forever young,
Forever young, forever young,
May you stay forever young.

May your hands always be busy,
May your feet always be swift,
May you have a strong foundation
When the winds of changes shift.
May your heart always be joyful,
And may your song always be sung,
May you stay forever young,
Forever young, forever young,
May you stay forever young.[14]

Chapter 2

Summer's Fullness: Finding Fulfillment in the Rising and Falling Phases of Life

When we were children, summer lasted forever. The days stretched out. The light lengthened. The world was playful, carefree, dream-like, endless. We were alive — with playmates real and imagined. And, at moments, we felt we could talk to the trees and the birds and all the other creatures above and below and around us. All were our kin. And this included all the elements: Wind in trees and in the tall grass. Waters of creek or stream, river or ocean. Rocks in gardens or on cliffs. The fiery sun. The languid clouds. The night sky, too. Everything companioned us. In a time out of time, where the heart ruled.

From this summer lyric, let us pick three images to dwell with: the **sun**, the **heart,** and **relational life**.

First, the *sun* with its light and warmth. Shining on all of us. Suggesting, in summer, fullness, fulfillment, completion. Nothing left out.

Second, the ***heart***, calling us to care for the communities in which we dwell — from friendships to family to larger communities. Wholeheartedly, to invite each of those communions to be heart whole.

A morning poem (gatha) from the community of Thich Nhat Hanh says:

> Waking up this morning, I smile
> Twenty-four brand new hours are before me.
> I vow to live fully in each moment
> and to look at all beings with eyes of compassion.[1]

The first line sounds the note of the heart — "waking up . . . I smile." Wakefulness and joy. The last line reminds us that the heart is in service of our life with others. In fact, the heart promises partnership — whether in the midst of joys or sorrows.

Third, our ***relational life*** extends the resonances of the sun and the heart. We might say: "In the beginning is relationship." We enter the world in the care of others and we learn to become, in our turn, caregivers. Again and again, we are reminded of how intertwined with others we are. We occupy a unique place in the great web of all life. Unique, yes. In the great web, yes. Holding both aspects simultaneously. As an ancient text expresses it:

> Heaven is my father and earth is my mother
> and even such a small creature as I
> find an intimate place in its midst.
>
> . . . .
>
> All people are my brothers and sisters
> And all things are my companions.[2]

So it was in the days of summer when we were children. Might it not be so again?

In this essay, I wish to explore three themes: (a) summer sun with its sense of fulfillment, (b) the heart with its care for the community, and (c) the primacy of relationship throughout. I wish to explore them as they are manifest in all the stages of our lives, but especially in the later years. So let us return to the four stages of life as articulated in ancient India: Student, Householder, Forest Dweller, and Sage.

- ❧ What might fulfillment mean for the Student-in-us?
- ❧ What might fulfillment mean for the Householder-in-us?
- ❧ What might fulfillment mean for the Forest Dweller-in-us?
- ❧ What might fulfillment mean for the Sage-in-us?

Put differently, what is maturity or completion at each stage? What is the quality of heart at each stage? What is the quality of relational understanding and love at each stage?

Recall that our life can be seen in two arcs: the arc of ascent and the arc of descent. In a calendar year, spring and summer mark ascending or rising energy; autumn and winter signal descending or falling energy. We are more familiar with thinking of fulfillment in the rising energy of a life (stages of Student and Householder); we are less practiced at understanding fulfillment in the falling energy of life (stages of Forest Dweller and Sage).

The Arc of Ascent — When Life Energy Is Rising

Part I: Summer Fulfillment for the Student-in-us

When I taught university students I held out the ideal of a lifelong love of learning. Of course, both love and learning must be present. This implies that the type of study must touch and enlarge the heart. I am pointing toward the "feeling intellect" or the "educated heart."[3] Dante speaks of an "intellectual light, light filled with love, love of true good, love filled with joy, joy surpassing every sweetness."[4]

Rumi also speaks of this type of knowing when he writes:

> There is a kind of Knowing that is a love.
> Not a scholarly knowing. That minutiae-collecting
> Doesn't open you. It inflates you, like a beard or a fancy turban.
> It announces you, saying,
> There are certain plusses and minuses
> which we must carefully consider.
> This other Knowing-Love is a rising light,
> a happiness in both worlds.[5]

Perhaps we could say that this love of learning is also a learning to love. Such study has a long history. In the monastic tradition, it was called *lectio divina* — a reflective and heart-felt tasting of the text for the sake of expanding and deepening our loves. So we begin with a type of reading — a type of study — that can nourish our soul and renew our spirit. Call it spiritual reading, yet the reality is much more.

What we read must refresh the spirit and hence will usually come from the wisdom traditions. Here we are keeping company with the true, the good, and the beautiful in thought and art. And keeping company with the great-souled ones among us.

How we read is equally important. The monastics spoke of tasting the words as if walking in the vineyard of the text.[6] Sapere = to taste. Sapientia = wisdom. All this echoes Psalm 34:8: "Taste and see that the Lord is good." When we read in this fashion, it becomes a spiritual practice. This sort of learning to love is complete with every enlargement of our capacity to receive our life. Fulfilled and complete in each moment, ever open to increase our longing.

Part II: Summer Fulfillment for the Householder-in-us

Summer shows up most intensely in the Householder. In other words, the sun, the heart, and life-in-relationship are at full strength in the Householder. Think first of the sun with its light and warmth. In one sense, the Student comes to completion in the Householder.[7] The student takes his or her place in the world, learns to care for a circle larger than him or herself. This, as already noted, is most often seen as a couple expands their love to include children. The space of family. The sense of intergenerational time. I come to see myself in the midst of generations — my parents and their parents and their parents, my children and their children and their children. The kingdom or "kindom"[8] spreads out in space and time.

Freud defined maturity as the ability to love and the ability to work. Such maturity is seen in the image of the Householder who takes on the care of a community and is aware of doing so. We can also imagine the Householder whose household is an institution — perhaps a college or corporation. We can imagine taking on responsibility in varying ways for still larger units — one's nation or one's planet. Indeed the word "ecology" derives from the Greek: "the study (logos) of one's *oikos* or home."

What is the fulfillment of the Householder? In one sense, the Householder is fulfilled in the children leaving home and taking on their own lives. In another sense, the family has simply changed form. As the shape of family shifts, new habits of heart and mind are called for to care for the whole and attend to its unique participants.

To have children, someone has said, is to live with your heart outside your body. Perhaps better, to live with our collective, familial heart outside our personal bodies. We have a new body and a new heart. Think of a garden where two apple trees grow. The garden is well placed to take advantage of sun and water. The other plants are well chosen to complement the two central trees.

Insects, birds, animals, and people visit the garden. Gardeners care for the whole. They know when the context of the whole garden is healthy. They know when the individual members of the garden are flourishing. Robert Irwin placed this inscription on the garden he designed for the J. Paul Getty Museum in Los Angeles:

> Always changing, never twice the same.

So it is with the garden of a friendship or a family or a college or corporation. The sun brings light and warmth. We who tend these gardens bring qualities of understanding and loving-kindness, wisdom, and compassion. The family then becomes a school of love inviting us to cultivate ways of coming to life more fully in all our relationships as they form and reform in kaleidoscope-like ways.

The Arc of Descent — When Life Energy Is Falling

Part I: Summer Fulfillment for the Forest Dweller-in-us

Consider the Autumn phase of life — after retirement, let us say. The children are grown and one form of tending is over. Perhaps parents move over to become grandparents. They have entered the arc of descent; they experience falling energy. Shall we regard it as positive descent or negative decline? How shall we be with this phase? Is there fulfillment in letting go and letting be? How might we think about that?

For most of our lives, we have thought of fulfillment in terms of achievement, success, fame, and fortune. Upward and onward. Our culture reinforces this pattern. Is there fulfillment in simplifying? In returning to nature and to elemental things? Can one have less and less of certain things and more and more of other things?

A famous Zen story tells of a Western professor coming to Japan to study Zen. He meets with a Zen master and the master pours tea. And continues to pour the tea. As the cup overflows and runs over the table, the professor exclaims: "Stop. Can't you see it's full?" The Zen master smiles. "That's how you are," he responds. "So full of your own beliefs and opinions. How can I teach you Zen?"

With Autumn comes acknowledging and letting go. Acknowledging life exactly as it is in its surface and depth. Acknowledging fundamental worth allows us to let go of what no longer serves — opinions and beliefs, ideas and identities, roles and self-concepts. Acknowledging deep value, we can let go of what is not essential to us after all. In letting go and letting be, there is stillness and a space to see. As the song from Godspell has it: "To

see Thee more clearly, to love Thee more dearly, to follow Thee more nearly — day by day."[9]

"My barn having burned, I can now see the moon." So the Zen tradition puts it. Perhaps I realize I am more than my costumes. I come to see myself as a unique reflection of the Great Mystery. Then I can become nothing — nothing special. And at the same time, everything. For I identify with all beings and rest in peace. Between nothing and everything, I am again something — one jewel in the great web of Indra (chief Hindu god) reflecting the whole from a particular, unrepeatable perspective.

Part II: Summer Fulfillment for the Sage-in-us

I want to introduce the Sage through a story:

> For several weeks strange sounds had drifted over the mountains from the neighboring valley. There was much talk in the village about what these noises could be, but no one could make sense of them. Even the village elders had never heard anything like them. Finally one of the young men of the village was chosen to cross the mountains and see what was going on.

After two days of hiking he reached the mountaintop and saw in the valley far below a hive of activity with dozens of people working. As he drew closer, he saw a line of people, each with a huge stone in front of them that they were hammering and chiseling.

When he finally reached the valley floor he approached a young man at one end of the line and asked, "What are you doing?"

"Huh!" grunted the young man. "I'm killing time until I get off work."

Puzzled, the hiker turned to the second person in the line, a young woman, and asked, "Excuse me, but what are you doing?"

"I'm earning a living to support my family," she responded.

Scratching his head, the hiker moved on to the third person and asked again, "What are you doing?"

"I'm creating a beautiful statue," came the reply. Turning to the next person, the hiker repeated his question.

"I'm helping to build a cathedral," came the answer.

"Ah!" said the hiker. "I think I'm beginning to understand." Approaching the woman who was next in line he asked, "And what are you doing?"

"I am helping the people in this town and generations that follow them, by helping to build this cathedral."

"Wonderful," exclaimed the hiker. "And you, sir?" he called to the man beside her.

"I am helping to build this cathedral in order to serve all those who use it and to awaken myself in the process. I am seeking my salvation through service to others."

Finally the hiker turned to the last stone worker, an old, lively person whose eyes twinkled and whose mouth formed a perpetual smile. "And what are you doing?" he inquired.

"Me?" smiled the elder. "Doing?" The elder roared with laughter. "This ego dissolved into God many years ago. There is no 'I' left to 'do' anything. God works through this body to help and awaken all people and draw them to Him."[10]

The elder of the story holds the key to fulfillment in the stage of sageliness. What has happened is that the illusions of earlier years — the quest to be somebody and to live in the eyes of others — drops away. Always you were loved. Always I was loved. Always we were at one with the Source. Nowhere to go, nothing to do. Or alternately, somewhere to go and something to do, yet not under illusion.[11] Seeing clearly. Acting joyfully. In alignment with the Great Work and the Great Love. So we might say: "I do not do the work for myself. I do not do the work by myself. I do not do the work with my own powers alone."

A Jew, thinking of our true size, might recall the teaching of Rabbi Simcha Bunim of Peshischa: "Everyone should have two pockets, each containing a slip of paper. On one should be written: 'I am but dust and ashes,' and on the other: 'For me, the world was created.' From time to time we must reach into one pocket, or the other. The secret of living comes from knowing when to reach into each."[12]

A Christian might say: "I live, now not I, but the Christ lives in me."[13] Or think of Jesus's daunting words to the rich young man: "Sell all you have. Give to the poor. . . . Come and follow me."[14]

Indeed there is something terrifying in truly practicing the presence of God. And something paradoxical as well. How crazy. We have everything and keep looking for more!

A Muslim might remember Abu Sa'id saying: "A true saint is one who walks amongst the people and eats and dwells with them and buys and sells in the market and marries and socializes yet never forgets God for a single moment."[15]

A Zen man or woman might say with Seng Ts'an: "When the ten thousand things are viewed in their oneness, we return to the Origin and remain where we have always been."

Eckhart Tolle, in speaking of surrender and finding God, puts all our themes together in these beautiful words: "Suddenly, a great stillness arises within you, an unfathomable sense of peace. And within that peace, there is great joy. And within that joy, there is love. And at the innermost core, there is the sacred, the immeasurable, That which cannot be named."[16]

A Taoist might smile or, with the sage of the cathedral builders, laugh out loud.

So the sages listen deeply to what is occurring within and around them. Not taking things personally, they are ready to act from a center beyond themselves, willing to reinforce movement where it is flowing well. Where is fulfillment here? It is paradoxically, Nowhere and Now Here.[17] And there is a further paradox as well. On the arc of descent, there is no one to take credit, so all moves effortlessly. The Sage can wear any costume and even play the fool.

Coda: Summer's Lessons

We began with three signs of Summer — the sun with its fulfillment. The heart caring for the whole. Everywhere seeing life as relationship, interconnection, interbeing.

First, we found that fulfillment was far from a once-for-all phenomenon. No fulfillment is the last word. We are:

- never finished with learning
- never finished with caring for our sectors of the Great Web of Life
- never finished with letting go and letting be, simplifying and returning to nature
- never finished with practicing the presence of God or, alternatively, getting out of our own way so that the greater light and love may shine through

Second, each season has a fulfillment on its own terms:

- The "heart learning" of the Student issues again and again in insight. As insight expands, so likewise does compassion. Each act of insight–compassion is cause for celebration.

- The caring of the Householder issues in the well-being of the unit and those within its enveloping field. Think of the task of parenting. Think of the marker events of achievements as the children grow in understanding and love and the parents grow as well. Each act of caring that reaches a fulfillment — however temporary — is cause for celebration.

- The acknowledgment and letting go of the Forest Dweller also has its fulfillment. Suppose that the Forest Dweller practices acknowledging and letting go of the three poisons: clinging, condemning, and identifying (with beliefs and roles, ideas and identities).[18] Suppose we notice we are clinging to a particular "story" — a particular way of seeing and speaking — that causes unnecessary suffering to ourselves and others. We let it go. Each act of such "letting go" brings clarity and freedom and is cause for celebration.

- The Sage practices the art of disappearing, in a paradoxical way. As more of my agenda falls away, there is more space for That Which Matters to show itself. Each moment of openness to the Mystery is an instance of grace and a cause for celebration. Paradoxically, I become more of what I truly am in thus opening to the universe.

Third, I can get better at each stage through practice. And there is a sequence here.

- The Student drops a certain amount of egocentricity to allow the learning to be itself.
- The Householder drops a certain amount of egocentricity to allow, say, the family to be itself and flourish.
- The Forest Dweller drops a certain amount of egocentricity by gaining skill in simplification, and hence the natural world becomes more itself.
- The Sage becomes more skillful at a deeper allowing — allowing and listening. And "all that is" flashes forth in glory.

"Me?" smiled the elder. "Doing?" The elder roared with laughter. "This ego dissolved into God many years ago. There is no 'I' left to 'do' anything. God works through this body to help and awaken all people and draw them to Him."

In such a Summer day, all is complete at every moment. And laughter rings out in celebration.

Chapter 3

Autumn's Way: Releasing and Simplifying

> And I rose
> In the rainy autumn
> And walked abroad in a shower of all my days.[1]

A shower of leaves falling on a rainy autumn day. A glory and a grieving. An exaltation of color, then a rain of leaves. See them showering down, as a quiet rain. See them falling as spray lifting off a waterfall and descending, releasing and returning to earth — to the earth that is their home and ours.

In Autumn we sense a turning of the year. The rising currents of Spring and Summer have reached their peak. The falling energy of Autumn and Winter appears. Return to an earlier question: How shall we approach this side of the cycle? Shall we see it as decline and diminution or as something else? I suggest that we approach this arc of descent under a number of descriptions:

1. Simplification and return to nature
2. Letting go and letting be — becoming aware of thoughts and feelings
3. Forgiving and being forgiven
4. Letting go and letting be — returning to the Source

We shall explore each in turn. But first a reminder. I have been taking the four stages of life from ancient India and overlaying them on the four seasons. In this picture, the stage of Forest Dweller appears in the midst of the downward and inward energy of Autumn.

We might summarize in this way: the arc of ascent from Student to Householder is about accomplishment, about doing and striving and achieving one's place in the world. The lure of fame and fortune urges us on. The arc of descent is about something else, a different energy, a different resting. We might think of it in this way:

- In the first half of life, we strive; in the second half we release from striving.
- In the first half of life, we seek to be somebody; in the second half we allow ourselves to be nobody (and perhaps — since we are less attached to one way of being and may understand others better — we may become, in a sense, everyman/ everywoman as well).

➥ In the first half of life, we look to power, prestige, and possessions to define us; in the second half we release from identifying with power and prestige and possessions. We allow ourselves to stand in the mystery of who we are as a unique reflection of all that is, already having all we seek, already being more than we can imagine.

The Autumn dynamic is similar to how Michelangelo spoke about sculpture. He said that making a sculpture was easy. All one had to do was find a block of marble in which the figure already existed and cut away what did not belong. In our case, even the metaphor of "cutting away" is too active. Perhaps better to say that we allow to fall away whatever was never who we really were nor are.[2]

1. The Call to Simplify and Return to Nature

Imagine the arc of descent beginning when a man or woman retires. In ancient India when one's work life is finished and the children leave home, a person was invited to move from Householder to Forest Dweller. The first invitation to the Forest Dweller is to reconnect with the natural world. This has always proved renewing. Think of contact with forest, with wilderness and wildness, with the

great ocean, with the sky-seeking mountains, with the vast stillness of the desert. To leave the bustle of city life and retreat to the more primal setting of nature itself.

A first practice in simplifying is to open our senses and reawaken our delight in simple things. Become reacquainted with the four elements dear to our ancestors: the earth, the water, the fire, the air. Examine rocks and minerals. Touch the good earth with its plants and trees. Realize that we, human ones, are companioned by the creatures of sea and earth and sky. All our kin. Surely this sense of situating ourselves in the great web of life, in the great family of all creatures, has never been more timely.

Poet Wendell Berry speaks of the healing powers of the natural world in his poem "The Peace of Wild Things":

> When despair for the world grows in me
> and I wake in the night at the least sound
> in fear of what my life and my children's lives may be,
> I go and lie down where the wood drake
> rests in his beauty on the water, and the great heron feeds.
> I come into the peace of wild things
> who do not tax their lives with forethought

of grief. I come into the presence of still water.
And I feel above me the day-blind stars
waiting with their light. For a time
I rest in the grace of the world, and am free.[3]

In the West, the gentle St. Francis of Assisi, in his "Canticle of the Sun," spoke of Brother Sun and Sister Moon, Brother Wind and Sister Water, Brother Fire and Mother Earth, and even Sister Death. His counterpart in the East, the beloved Japanese Zen monk, Ryōkan Taigu, loved playing with the children and delighted with all forms of life. His death poem was this: "showing their backs, then their fronts, falling maple leaves."[4]

We do not have to retreat to forest or mountains or ocean to return to nature. We can awaken to the beauty of simple things around us and within us. Indeed, the call for elders who are earth elders has never been more pressing. Two monastics in our time sound similar notes. Thich Nhat Hanh speaks of "interbeing," and writes:

> If you are a poet, you will see clearly that there is a cloud floating in this sheet of paper. Without a cloud, there will be no rain; without rain, the trees cannot grow; without trees, we cannot make paper. . . . So we can say that the cloud and

the paper *inter-are*. "Interbeing" is a word that is not in the dictionary yet, but if we combine the prefix "inter-" with the verb "to be," we have a new verb, inter-be.[5]

Thomas Berry, also a monastic, speaks of the need in our time to shift from seeing nature as *a collection of objects* to seeing nature as a *communion of subjects*.[6] Thus, the Forest Dweller both returns to simple elemental things and sees these beings as fellow creatures, as part of one's own Great Family, able to be encountered as having an interior as well as exterior life.

First, a simplification. A return to the present and the presence of Mystery at each moment. As the poet e. e. cummings says, "Now the eyes of my eyes are open, now the ears of my ears awake." Opening the senses in the present moment — this is one invitation to become Forest Dweller.

Second, a release that allows expansion. As we become less attached to roles and duties, ideologies and identities, the canvas of who we are can expand to include all our brothers and sisters and all our kin. This is a first paradox of releasing. The more I let go of specific definitions, the more freely and deeply I can participate with all beings. As we shed roles and identities to enter the zero point, we find we are already in a great communion or community. The Roman playwright Terence said: "I am a human being and nothing that is human is alien to me." This is a beautiful embrace of the entire human family. The Forest Dweller can say more: "I am a unique participant in the web of all life and nothing in this circle is alien to me." Willing to become nobody, I find I have become, in a certain sense, everybody.

2. Letting Go and Letting Be — Becoming Aware of Thoughts and Feelings

Two Zen stories from among my favorites emphasize letting go. The first is a story I told earlier, in chapter 2:

> A Western professor comes to visit a Japanese Zen master. The Zen master pours him tea. The tea begins to spill over the top of the cup and onto the table. Finally, the professor can stand it no longer. "Can't you see it's full?" he cries.

> The Zen master pauses. And with the hint of a twinkle in his eye says: "That is the way you are. So full of your own opinions, beliefs, certainties. How can I teach you Zen?"

The invitation: Empty the cup. And the image here of emptiness is a central one to the Buddhist tradition. Let us explore it step by step. What needs emptying? The mind and heart. Emptying of what? From the mind: Old ideas, beliefs, opinions, certainties, identities. From the heart: clinging, condemning, and identifying (identifying with our attachments and our aversions).

A second Zen story goes like this:

> Once upon a time, two Zen monks were returning to their monastery after a long journey. As they came upon a swift running stream, a lovely young woman came toward them from a grove of trees where she had been waiting. "Noble sirs," she said, "I am traveling to aid my mother who has fallen ill. She lives across the stream and to the south. But the stream is so swollen that I cannot cross for fear I shall be swept away. Will you help me cross, good sirs?"
>
> The elder of the two monks nodded graciously, picked up the young woman, and carried her across the raging stream. On the other side, he lowered her gently to the ground. The young woman expressed her thanks and continued on her way toward the south. The two monks wished her well and turned

to the north to continue their journey home. Neither spoke for an hour. Then the younger of the two said to his companion: "I have been wondering: Do you think that it is right and proper for us who are monks to touch a young lady, especially one so beautiful as she?" The elder monk smiled and said: "I lifted her up and put her down an hour ago. You are still carrying her."

In all inner work, we can distinguish between (1) what is happening and (2) how we are relating to what is happening. We relate to something in two main ways:

🌿 51 🌿

- ☙ Through our intellectual meaning-making (how we understand, interpret, "language" life)
- ☙ Through our emotional value-creating (our liking or disliking, our attachments or aversions, our desires and fears, greed and anger)

Then, alas, we lock in our meaning-making and our value-creating by telling ourselves "That's just the way I am (or he/she is, or they are, or the situation is)."

Yet, we can learn to observe our language and observe our emotional responses — how we name things and how we generate

desire and fear, allure and anger. We are meaning-makers and value-creators. On each of these poles, we can become fixed and fixated.

Still, there is hope. If we create the conversations in which we live, we can alter those conversations. We can let go of small-minded conversations and replace them with larger-minded conversations. If we generate our emotional responses to people and situations, we can alter those emotional responses. We can let go of small-minded, suffering-causing responses and substitute larger-minded, more beneficial responses.

In the story of the two monks and the beautiful woman, the elder monk represents the larger-minded possibilities in us. The younger monk represents the smaller-minded possibilities in us. Constricted thought forms, larger thought forms. Ego-centered emotional projections or compassionate empathy. If we are awake and alert, we can choose. Opening the mind and opening the heart gives everyone more room to be.

3. Forgiving and Being Forgiven — With More Room to Be

Letting go — as the waterfall releases the water, allowing it to fall joyously — airborne now, and still on its way to the sea. In this movement, this current, I see the Forest Dweller participating in

Autumn. Having released old stories and let go of greedy, angry emotions, something ever ancient and ever new appears.

When I release from identifying with my thoughts, with my ideologies and identities, then what lies at the depth in you and in me has a chance to become manifest. I see the dancer and the dance. I see the inner light, and bliss enters quietly.

We return to what is. And that is perhaps the most challenging of statements. Who are we and what is going on within and around and among us? I think of each person and situation as having a surface, a mid-point, and a depth. "What is" must be a large enough context to acknowledge the surface difficulties and the mid-level observations and the mysterious depth that has many names and no name.

Let us apply the lessons of Autumn to our relations with our parents. All parents gift and wound their children — our parents gifted and wounded us and we gifted and wounded our own children. Furthermore, our dialogue with our parents — living or dead, in spoken words or in our heads — is never finished. Throughout our lives, we are comparing and sorting out. As we get older, as we have children, we may return to our parents with a bit more compassion. How young they were when they had us. How much they dreamed of how it would be. Gifts and

wounds. As we get older, as we have our own children, we begin to recognize that:

- Some of what we once called "wounds" turned out to have been "gifts in disguise."
- Some of what we once called "gifts" turned out to be "wounds in disguise."

So I propose that we seek to forgive our parents. As we forgive our parents, we will find that we are forgiving ourselves at the same time.

- Forgiving our parents for not being all they wished to be — for being often unskillful or confused.
- Forgiving our parents for not being all we wished them to be.
- Forgiving ourselves for asking the impossible of our parents and perhaps also of ourselves.

By forgiving parents I mean to recognize that they, like us, are limited human beings, often unskillful, not always able to bring about what they wished to do or be. When we let go of the impossible dream of perfection, when we drop our shifting — often conflicting — measuring rods, we may notice that in their very particularity, in their very struggle, our parents have a unique glory — one always there yet unnoticed by us except in moments. Perhaps we see anew the sacrifices they made and the persistence they showed.

To forgive in this context is to bow to parents exactly as they are at the surface and at the depth. It is to recognize in them all their surface disturbances, fears and uncertainties, hopes and dreams, weaknesses and avoidances. And it is to recognize their deep nature, their full unique beauty. It has been said that, for each of us, there is —in the other world —a stone with our true name on it. And we do not even know that name. To see our parents as God sees them is to see both their surface disturbances and their unique, unrepeatable beauty and inestimable worth. To see them as sacred and also imperfect.

No matter how often we see or remember our parents, we can always return anew. We can drop the old stories. We can come to them with a larger heart and more compassionate eyes. How do we enlarge our hearts or, to change the metaphor, how do we polish the mirror of the heart so that we may see more of what is there? One master said: "To polish the heart, smile and speak in kindly ways."[7] We can commit ourselves to doing that, right here and right now with regard to our parents — to smile and to speak in kindly ways.

If our parents are with us still, we can do that in their presence. If they are no longer with us, we can do that in their absence.

4. Letting Go and Letting Be: Returning to the Source

Perhaps a "releasing moment" is joined with every "acting moment." First, we practice acknowledging situations and people exactly as they are in surface and depth. The practice of releasing — of letting go — moves us to equanimity, to a state where we are able to be more attentive to our brothers and sisters and less blinded by our personal karmic formations. The Buddhist tradition speaks of the Four Immeasurable Abodes or Minds: *love (or loving-kindness)*, *compassion*, *joy (or sympathetic joy)*, and *equanimity*.[8] All are interdependent. When we practice one deeply, the rest come along with it. Love deepens when it is sensitive to suffering and joy and finds a serenity in facing whatever comes. Compassion is enriched by love and joy and equanimity. And so for each. Yet in Autumn, I wish to speak especially of equanimity — a loving, compassionate, joyful equanimity.

Meister Eckhart, the fourteenth-century mystic, instructs us to think of equanimity as a hinge.[9] The door swings back and forth but the hinge remains steady and constant and unmoved.

Equanimity is both the practice and the fruit of letting go. It is to face whatever comes as containing a way through. Rumi's poem "The Guest House" points the way:

> This being human is a guest house.
> Every morning a new arrival.
> A joy, a depression, a meanness,
> some momentary awareness comes
> as an unexpected visitor.
> Welcome and entertain them all!
> Even if they are a crowd of sorrows,
> who violently sweep your house
> empty of its furniture,
> still, treat each guest honorably.
> He may be clearing you out
> for some new delight.
> The dark thought, the shame, the malice.
> Meet them at the door laughing
> And invite them in.
> Be grateful for whatever comes,
> because each has been sent
> as a guide from beyond.[10]

If we meet each with love, with compassion, with joy, then surely
equanimity will arise. In equanimity, we shall touch all four abodes
in the face of whatever arrives.

Yet there is a further movement — link it with letting be. This
is a state wherein we rest at the Source of all. Union, communion,
unity, community, all are present. Or in a different narrative, God
and humankind and all beings are experienced as a oneness and we
are that.[11] As the old Bedouin said to Lawrence of Arabia: "The
love is from God and of God and towards God."[12] And we may
enter the stream — where? There! Anywhere! At each moment
and in each place. We can enter the stream and allow the deeper
waters to bathe us through and through.

In a first draft of releasement, we do the releasing and we create
that which we release. In a deeper sense, we neither create the
obstacles nor do we do the releasing. No "I." No "Thou." Nothing
to release! Autumn is moving to the depth of Winter waters. And,
in the waters, we catch a glimpse of the Sage-in-us.

The Zen Master Seng Ts'an offers a hint as he reminds us,
"When the ten thousand things are viewed in their oneness, we
return to the Origin and remain where we have always been."[13]

Chapter 4

Winter's Gifts: Dwelling in the Depth

Here is a poem by Juan Ramón Jiménez called "Oceans":

> I have a feeling that my boat
> has struck, down there in the depths,
> against a great thing.
> And nothing
> happens! Nothing . . . Silence . . . Waves . . .
> — Nothing happens? Or has everything happened,
> and are we standing now, quietly, in the new life?[1]

Among the ancient Chinese, Winter is associated with the deep waters. Let the image sink in. Winter and the deep waters. Think of moonlight over the ocean in winter. Moonlight across the waters in the depth of night. Silence. Solitude. Stillness. Darkness and deep listening. Dwelling at the depth and truly not-knowing. All mysterious. "Darkness was over the deep waters and the Spirit was hovering over the waters."[2]

Such vastness, such realms of the unknown, produce fear. Our ancestors felt this fear. Could we get through the winter? Would there be a new year? Would renewed life return? The clue is in the image itself. In deep waters, the surface may be stirred up, yet at the depth there is peace and calm. All proceeds according to its own nature and norms. So we may find, beneath fear, a more basic trust. "Fear not" is the biblical message.

What sort of trust lies at the depth? Not the trust that comes with sight — neither foresight nor hindsight. Rather it is a trust that lives in the darkness, that learns to navigate without sight. Relinquishing sight, we rely on hearing. We sense the subtle rhythms by listening deeply. Winter encourages the practice of deep listening — listening to what is said and unsaid, to the sounds and the silence between the sounds.

"Johnny," said the first grade teacher, "you're not paying attention."

"Yes I am," replied Johnny. "I'm paying attention to everything."

What would it be like to listen attentively to everything? As if everything was laden with meaning. As if everything was a teacher for those with ears to hear.

Suppose that we think of the atmosphere as an invisible ocean. We might think of ourselves as already living within the ocean. Rumi writes:

> Late by myself, in the boat of myself
> no light and no land anywhere, cloud cover thick
> I try to stay just above the surface, yet
> I'm already under and living within the ocean.[3]

Anne Joy, the 5-year-old daughter of a colleague, was sitting out on the porch with her father on a July evening. They were watching a storm come in. She suddenly said, "Sometimes I think about things. Like: why am I in this world? I could be in a different world . . ."[4]

I would gloss my young friend's remarks in this way: The different world can be this world seen in a different way. If we are awake and alert, we always have the choice: Will we live in a world that is conditioned and constricted by personal and collective patterns? Or will we begin to notice those structures and realize that they are just part of the story, just part of the movie? We could be living in a different world — a larger, deeper world — a world beneath the surface certainties, a paradoxical world — in time and beyond time.

"There is another world and it lies within this one."[5] So speaks Paul Eluard. I think of a deeper dimension, the inside of the inside of things. To discover this dimension may be like awakening from a black-and-white world into Technicolor. Or like hearing more subtle music in the midst of the ordinary. Our relentless and often ruthless certainties are suddenly understood to be illusory — lines drawn on water, pretending to be fixed.[6] They fall away. Something new stands before us.

The mystics tell us that, if we shift our interpretive frame, the deeper world (or deeper dimension of this world) will manifest all about us. Here is a slight rephrasing of William Blake's quote: "If the doors of perception were cleansed, everything would appear to us as it is, infinite. For we have closed ourselves up, till we see all things through narrow chinks of our cavern."[7]

Winter invites us to open the doors of hearing, to open a third ear, to listen in a new way. Suppose that we are always living in a story (which we take to be real). Seeing our life *as a story* invites us to take that story less literally and to live more lightly. "It is only a movie," we say. So likewise, we can say, "It is only a story." Here the "only" allows certitudes to fall away, or at least be loosened. Once we confront our lives as a story then we may ask: What kind of a story are we co-creating? A faith story? An emerging universe story? A tragedy or a comedy? How can we listen to life-as-story in such a way as to reveal the mysterious and liberating layers of what is said and what is unsaid, of the tones and overtones?

When I engage in the ancient art of storytelling, I ask my listeners to follow three guidelines:

1. **Approach each aspect of "the story" as having multiple layers of meanings.**

   Avoid seeking one moral of the story. Let the story remain richer than any one interpretation. Indeed, what we know is incomplete, and what we can tell is even more unfinished, more provisional.

2. **Consider that you are all the characters in the story** — the one you think of as yourself plus all the other characters, the main ones, the supporting players, even the villains.

   Understood in this way, the characters in the story reveal parts of you. They come to you (mostly unknown to themselves) as teachers, perhaps even as severe teachers[8] who have wronged you in myriad ways. We might say,

shifting an old aphorism: When you listen with the ears of a student, all things teach you.

3. **Think of the story as a commentary on your current life,** as happening here and now in support of your own transformation and that of others.

In this way, story becomes parable and directs us to a deeper and more meaningful life in the present moment and in the presence of Mystery.

Deep listening opens a world that is soul size. Here we might think of soul not as an individual possession but as an individual participation in the World Soul — something our ancestors glimpsed. Imagine this "soul of the world" the way our ancestors did — as Sophia, a wisdom that connects through love. In this fashion, the "ocean" in which we dwell is an ocean of meaning and value, an ocean of insight and love. We might speak of living in and from the Soul of the World. We might speak of living in the nurturing Spirit. Whether called soul dimension or spirit dimension, we come to it through letting go of old identities, old opinions (personal and collective), and listening to what lies deeply within and around us.

Sometimes, in whatever way it comes to us, we may have a sense of the glory all around us.[9] Blessed are such times. At other times, we may feel, as the opening poem said, that nothing is happening. Then we practice a trust even in the dark times. A trust that each event has many meanings. That each being is a teacher in disguise. That our living is in service of our transformation and that of others.

Winter encourages the discipline of waiting — in trust, in faithfulness, in hopefulness, in love. Silence. Solitude. Stillness. Soul. Spirit. Signs of the deep waters.

T. S. Eliot teaches that again and again we return "to where we started and know the place for the first time." We return to the beginning, to "the source of the longest river, the voice of the hidden waterfall and the children in the apple tree." They are "not known, because not looked for but heard, half-heard, in the stillness between two waves of the sea." "Quick now, here, now, always — A condition of complete simplicity (Costing not less than everything). And all shall be well and all manner of thing shall be well . . ."[10]

The true gift of Winter, I am coming to understand, is unknowing. This unknowing is very different from ignorance. It is more like the ability to hear the story anew — with loving attention to the concrete details, with awareness that all the details and all the

characters have something to reveal to me. And further, this listening is a holy listening. For I am not in the story passively; I am, with the storyteller, uncovering insight and renewing life in the ever-surprising present. For example, part of my story may be the view that my colleague Paul is rude to me. Yet as I live more deeply and symbolically, I may play with what the wonderful Byron Katie calls "the turn around." How am I rude to Paul? How am I rude to myself? How is Paul not rude to me?[11]

Then a part of my story re-forms, deepens. Perhaps laughter and lightness return. Perhaps the Sage-in-us appears as the Fool, happily deconstructing old certainties and allowing new possibilities to shine forth.[12]

The gifts of Winter are always available — to listen deeply in unknowing to what is unfolding at the surface and in the depth. Yet they have a special place as we draw closer to death. Earlier in life, we live through the death of each season, as we live through the death of Winter into Spring. And we may neglect the downward and inward side of life in a rush to define ourselves by outward "doing." We may fail to honor the Winter energy of stillness and silence and solitude and simplicity as we rush about seeking to construct our life. Yet these very qualities beckon more insistently as we move closer to death.

Rabbi Zalman Schachter-Shalomi speaks of life in a biblical perspective of seven-year intervals. And he maps those intervals onto the months of the year. In this fashion, October looks to ages 63–70, November to ages 70–77, and December to ages 77–84 and beyond.[13] These are the Winter years or Autumn–Winter years in a lifetime. In his eighties, Reb Zalman is in his December years. And he speaks these days of being drawn to solitude and the contemplative life. In these later years, contemplative practices call us. It does not mean that we need to withdraw from the world. It does mean that we cultivate, more and more, a different world. Being silent, we listen and, even in speaking, we can speak in a listening mode. In action, we have the opportunity for what I will call "trim-tab living."

Buckminster Fuller called our attention to the trim tab. He was thinking of a great ocean liner like the Queen Mary. He remembered that the ship is steered with a rudder and, at the edge of the rudder, is a kind of miniature rudder called a trim tab. A small movement of the trim tab causes the rudder to move and, as the rudder turns, the entire ship turns. Buckminster Fuller thought of himself as a trim tab.[14] I would say that any of us — by attunement to the currents — can engage in trim-tab living.

In trim-tab living, we live more simply and yet more powerfully because we do not rely upon our own powers alone. Listening to what is unfolding in the deep, in the "not yet manifest" realm, we say a word. Or omit a comment. And we do this with loving intent. As we align our thoughts and words and actions with the deeper life we sense, as we participate in the great story unfolding, we bestow Winter's gifts and are at peace.

If we dwell in the story told by the religions of the book,[15] we image the ultimate in a personal manner. Then we can say in listening to the deep story anew: "Ah, you appear like that. Ah, you appear like this. Everywhere there is the face of faces, veiled as in a mystery."[16]

Here also we might say with Dante, "And His will is our peace [E sua voluntade è nostra pace]. It is that sea to which all moves that it creates or nature makes."[17]

In the East, one can also image the ultimate in a non-personal manner and call it, for example, the Tao (pronounced "dow"). The Tao is the Way of the universe. We glimpse the Tao in meditative mind, in nature, and in the appearance of the Masters, the large-souled ones. Here is how the storyteller (Lao Tzu) speaks of these masters in the Tao Te Ching (the Classic of the Power of the Way):

The ancient masters were subtle, mysterious, profound, responsive.
The depth of their knowledge is unfathomable,
All we can do is describe their appearance.

[How do they appear?]

Watchful, like those crossing a winter stream.
Alert, like men and women aware of danger.
Courteous, like visiting guests,
Yielding, like ice about to melt.
Simple like uncarved blocks of wood.
Hollow, like caves.
Opaque, like muddy pools.

[And what is the teaching for us?]

Who can wait quietly while the mud settles?
Who can remain still until the moment of action?
Observers of the Tao do not seek fulfillment.
Not seeking fulfillment, they are not swayed by change.[18]

Have we not here other pointers to Winter's gifts? To a way of dwelling at the depth of life? Do we not have further hints of how the Forest Dweller tends toward the deeper realms of the joyous Sage?

So, in light of these reflections, hear anew the poem with which we began —Juan Ramón Jiménez's "Oceans":

I have a feeling that my boat
has struck, down there in the depths,
against a great thing.
And nothing
happens! Nothing . . . Silence . . . Waves . . .
— Nothing happens? Or has everything happened,
and are we standing now, quietly, in the new life?[19]

Afterword

Happiness is here and now,
I have dropped my worries.
Nowhere to go, nothing to do
No longer in a hurry.
Happiness is here and now,
I have dropped my worries.
Somewhere to go, something to do,
But I don't need to hurry.[1]

Returning to the Overture

In the Introduction, I mentioned three functions of elders:

- To keep the little things little and the big things big
- To encourage creativity (in oneself and others)
- To bless the young[2]

These functions are reminiscent of what good grandparents do.
I am thinking of those grandparents who themselves have become

elders through the gifts of Autumn and Winter. Such grandmothers or grandfathers help younger people:

- "Keep the little things little and the big things big" —
  - By holding in mind (what youth does not know) that "This too shall pass."
  - By letting go of the small and petty, the grandparents allow what is significant to appear.
- "Encourage creativity" —
  - By encouraging youth not to be fearful, to take risks, to live their own lives, to follow their hearts. Aiding the young to let go of obstacles, the grandparents help the young rediscover their hearts' desires.
- "Bless the young" —
  - By letting each one know that she or he is unique in all the world, of inestimable worth and beautiful beyond measure. Thus, the young are released from social or cultural definitions that are too small to live in.

Young people often see such vital elders as allies, if not co-conspirators.

Clearly, one does not become the kind of person in whose presence these three benefits occur merely by growing older. Growing older is no guarantee of growing as a person. We may instead become the kind of old folks who blame and complain and bother people — all the while singing about "the good old days!" How then does one become an elder who can keep the little things little and the big things big, encourage creativity, and bless the young?

Themes of the Book Revisited

In preparation to become an elder, I offered the reader:

1. A walk through the seasons to begin to grasp and live out their gifts
2. An overlay of the four stages (or functions) of life from ancient India
3. More basic than either, the notion of an arc of ascent (Spring–Summer or Student–Householder) and an arc of descent (Autumn–Winter or Forest Dweller–Sage).[3]

First, I presented the four seasons as a cycle:

- ❧ Spring begins
- ❧ Summer completes
- ❧ Autumn releases
- ❧ Winter waits

Second, I presented the stages of life, not as time spans but each having its own task or function:

- ❧ The Student's task is learning, and more specifically, learning those skills of mind and heart to become a Householder and take his or her place in the wider society.
- ❧ The Householder's task is to learn to care for the community where the community is of various sizes: couples, families, organizations (e.g., economic, educational, governmental, religious, etc.) all the way to the web of all life on the planet embedded in the universe.
- ❧ The Forest Dweller's task is to acknowledge and let go, to simplify and return to nature.

- The Sage's task is to become more and more attuned to forces larger than self, attuned to the widest and deepest horizon however named — the Great Mystery of all that is and all that matters.

Of course, in each of the phases of life all the seasons are present.

- Spring's arts of beginning anew,
- Summer's practices of caring for the communities given us,
- Autumn's practices of acknowledging and letting go, and
- Winter's practices of dwelling in the depth, opening ourselves to the Great Mystery, and practicing "trim-tab" living.

Third, I set both models against more primal currents which I called the arc of ascent and the arc of descent. The two arcs establish two different musical "keys of life" — outward and upward in the Spring–Summer years, downward and inward in the Autumn–Winter years.[4] The themes of ascent are not the themes of descent. The practices needed for outward and upward success

in the outer world involve effort, time, and steps. These practices
draw on the powers of Spring and Summer. The practices needed
for inward deepening involve releasing from illusions, letting go
of striving, tapping into forces greater than our own efforts, and
coming to realize over and over that we have all we seek and
that we are already home. These practices draw on the powers
of Autumn and Winter. This side of the cycle emphasizes (1)
receiving, (2) releasing, and (3) remembering.

    I have written the essays from the vantage point of a person
interested in becoming an elder, the perspective of one wanting to
enter the arc of descent in conscious, peaceful, and joyful ways. I
am exploring the opportunities of this phase myself. I am delighted
to have the companionship of fellow explorers.

The Circle Becomes a Spiral Path

The circle can become a spiral path of deepening. We not only circle round and round like a hawk in the thermals, we also grow and deepen. We learn life lessons. We revisit older wisdom to make it our own. Imagine in the center of the circle a vertical dimension stretching between heaven and earth. After each turn of the wheel of the seasons, we can return to center, integrate what we have learned, and deepen who we are and how we see everything. In other words, imagine a spiral moving from surface to depth.

What takes us to a new level is a new capacity for *"wise insight/ loving response."* With each turn, if we are moving constructively, our awareness deepens, our love expands, our commitment to continue strengthens.[5] Detaching from unhelpful ways in which we identify with our stories, we grow in wisdom and compassion. And we go round again, being a beginner at a new level, learning new relational skills, acknowledging and letting go of more subtle obstacles, and resting in the deep waters with greater awareness of the whole and our participation in the greater life.

Here is an analogy that I have found useful: States of awareness and loving response are like the levels of a lake.[6]

Let me invite you to a fantasy trip. Imagine that your core self detaches from your body and floats effortlessly out over your present city, out over a primal forest. In the distance, you see a lake. A gentle breeze stirs the waters. There are ripples on the surface of the lake. Suppose you touch down and become a ripple self. You think in ripple ways, with ripple worries, ripple concerns, making ripple comparisons and so on. At this level of non-awareness, you are asleep in your life, enslaved by old habits, with no space between incoming stimulus and outgoing response — the very definition of being reactive. You are embedded in a collective trance and do not realize that this is the case.[7]

Now imagine that, on the surface of the lake, you continue your ripple life. However, a part of you detaches from your ripple self and descends into the lake, coming to rest at the mid-level of the lake. You are completely safe under the water. You breathe easily. You can turn in any direction, like an astronaut in weightlessness. You even find you can let the water cradle you as if in a hammock. You can look up, from below, and see your ripple self on the surface caught in the cultural trance of fear and desire. Your gaze is a loving one. No harsh judgment. Rather you are filled with compassion for this "little you" who has served you diligently, if often unskillfully. You are watching yourself as a ripple much as you would watch a cartoon version of yourself, with detachment and gentle humor, with love and compassion.

Certain wisdom traditions name this "middle-level-of-the-lake" state. They call it your "observing self"[8] — that part of you that, with practice, can observe not only *what is happening*, but also (a) *how you are interpreting* and (b) *how you are emotionally responding* to what is before you. When you call forth this observing self (or listening self,) you find you have some distance from your thoughts and emotions. You are not your thoughts, and you are not your emotions. You generate thoughts; you generate emotions. You "have" thoughts and emotions, you are not identified with your thoughts and emotions. In the mode of observing self, you reduce the amount of clinging and condemning and identifying in your life. The Autumn energy of letting go and letting be is key. As you notice your stories and notice your reactivity, as you realize that they are only stories, only emotional states, you gain some freedom to shift your language and to choose your response.[9]

Now with your ripple self still on the surface and your observing self at the mid-level, imagine that again a part of you disengages and moves toward the depth of the lake. Here you navigate more

by listening than by sight. You begin to hear longer rhythms as if
the lake is connected to the great ocean and you are sensing deeper
and more subtle currents. Perhaps, in an instant, you realize that
all is water — the depth and the mid-level and the surface ripples.
All is one and you are that! How foolish to think of yourself as
separate! How clear at this moment that "yours" and "mine" are
but marks on water.

The key to this further descent is the Winter energy that moves
us into a creative unknowing and allows us to listen more deeply.
And we are still relying on the gravitational force of the downward
arc.

At the depth we are companions to the sages and saints, the
mystics and poets, the lovers and fools, the great-souled ones
known and unknown. Here we are learning to live as the sage
among the cathedral builders — the one who smiles and says "Me?
Doing? This ego dissolved into God many years ago. There is no
'I' left to 'do' anything. God works through this body to help and
awaken all people and draw them to Him."

The lessons of earlier stages of life remain with us — their
gifts, their wounds, and what we make of them. Having been
students, we can be learners still. More powerfully, we can practice

approaching each situation in beginner's mind. Having been Householders, we have already expanded our circle of care to units larger than our individual self alone. We can enter elderhood (Forest Dweller and Sage) with an awareness that we live in the midst of seven generations and that we are called upon to honor the ancestors and serve the children.[10]

As we come down the mountain, the force of gravity is with us. Spirituality in the stages of Forest Dweller and Sage is less about building up and more about letting go. The insight is that we already have all we need. Coming down the mountain, we are coming home. The sacred realm is within us and also around us, if we have eyes to see and ears to hear. The sacred is close at hand, ever present. We need only drop certain stories and beliefs, certain fears and hopes. As we do, we find we are already home. Nowhere to go, nothing to do. No longer in a hurry. And when there is "somewhere to go and something to do," we still don't have to hurry. We act within the power of the greater whole.

In the arc of descent, we are not building up an ego; we are disassembling an ego in service of possibilities less defined by society. We let go of the motivations of seeking fame and fortune whether material or spiritual. We are shaken by the realization that

in going to zero we are standing in full openness to the Mystery which enhances our worth and carries us along.

Poet Robert Bly presents as a poem these lines from an Inuit woman shaman:

> The great sea
> Has sent me adrift,
> It moves me as the weed in a great river,
> Earth and the great weather move me,
> Have carried me away
> And move my inward parts with joy.[11]

We become nobody or nobody special. We decrease so that other aspects may be made manifest in and through us.

Forest Dweller reminds us of the call to simplification and return to nature. Sage calls us to let go and let be in even more profound ways. In the deep waters, we align with the power of the Way. We are encouraged to become transparent so that the grace of the Holy One may work in and through us. We are invited to resonate with the powers of wholeness manifesting throughout the universe.

❧   ❧   ❧   ❧   ❧

Interlude

Some Practices for the Autumn and Winter Years

Receiving — Practices from the Center

Begin each interaction with gratitude (gratefulness or great fullness)

Shift from language of lack to language of sufficiency (even abundance)

Mantra: I have all I need, in myself and those who companion me, to live a life of quality right here and right now.

Releasing — Practices from Autumn's Gifts

First Release — into the mid-level of the lake — "dropping" into your observing self.

> Notice when you are in small mind (creating unnecessary suffering and less possibility for all), realize you have a choice, shift to larger mind-and-heart (creating less unnecessary suffering and more possibility for all).

Let go of conversations too small to live in. (e.g., conversations where you are holding on to things being your way or conversations where you are investing too much energy in opposition to what is).[12]

Let go of falsely believing that you are your stories and moods. Avoid saying "That's just the way I am (or he or she is or they are)."

Second Release — into the depth of the lake — dissolving your sense of separateness.

Release further your identification with stories and emotional charges, both those that are predominantly personal or part of one's cultural trance. Such releasing is aided by meditation and making friends with silence.

Mantra:

> I do not do the Great Work for myself alone —
> I do not do the Great Work by myself alone —
> I do not do the Great Work with my own powers alone.[13]

Remembering — Practices from Winter's Gifts

The practices of Winter are associated with the deep ocean and the capacity to listen deeply.

In the deep waters, my boundaries become more permeable, as if the great ocean flows in me and through me. I tap into the deeper currents and move freely. In the deep waters I participate in the community of the living, the dead, and those not yet born.

First, practice deep listening and mindful speaking — listening to what is said and unsaid, in the words and in the silence.[14]

Second, remember your deep nature and how it is connected with the whole.

Remember who you are at surface, midpoint, and depth.

Remember who others are at surface, midpoint, and depth.

Remember how we are all interconnected to one another and to the Source of our being.

The Religions of the book would have us remember we are created in the image and likeness of God. Then we are asked to love God (the One) with all our mind and soul and strength and our neighbor as ourselves.

When I image the Ultimate (and all there is) without name and form, I dwell in the Great Mystery with no name and many names.

When I image the Ultimate as an impersonal force like the Tao, I place myself in alignment with the longer rhythms of the universe unfolding.

When I image the Ultimate as a person, I seek union with the Holy One as a Thou who loves me and whom I love. Then, in the words of St. Richard of Chichester (set to music in the play Godspell) I seek:

> To know Thee more clearly,
> to love Thee more dearly,
> to follow Thee more nearly day by day.

More and more I allow the whole to act through me unto the good of all our kin.

I dwell in the love that the old Bedouin declared to Lawrence of Arabia, saying: "The love is from God and in God and towards God."

❦   ❦   ❦   ❦   ❦

Turning and Returning

Now, having finished the book, you are ready to begin again. Turning and turning on the spiral path. Turning and returning. In the initiation of fire — from Student to Householder, we learn to be with the rising energy of life, drawing upon the gifts of Spring and Summer. In the Night Sea Journey into elderhood, we learn how to be with the descending energies of life, drawing upon the gifts of Autumn and Winter. As we learn how to be with life both in its waxing and its waning, we glimpse something of the arts of living and dying.

Once again, as in times past, the ocean is calling those who are ready. Calling them to become Forest Dwellers. Calling them to dare to touch the Sage within. The sea is calling us to a simpler and a more contemplative life. To return to where we have always been. To know the place for the first time. As has been said:

> There is a polish for everything
> and the polish for the heart
> is remembrance of the One.[15]

Notes

Introduction

1   In modern life, the proportions seem to have these rough lineaments: about 20 years Student, 40 years Householder, and 20 years Elder (Forest Dweller and Sage). This is why the British tend to speak of retirement years as the Third Age. Still and all, I emphasize throughout that the arc of ascent (the upward and outward phase) is fundamentally different from the arc of descent (the downward and inward phase).

2   I first heard of these three functions from poet Robert Bly who applied them, in a mythic sense, to kings and queens. They have seemed to me apt functions for elders.

3   The poem is by Wu-men (1183–1260). The translation is by Stephen Mitchell. See Stephen Mitchell, *The Enlightened Heart* (New York: Harper & Row, 1989), p. 47.

Chapter 1

1   I am quoting the last lines of e. e. cummings' well-known poem "I thank You God for most this amazing day." See *Selected Poems of E. E. Cummings*, ed. Richard S. Kennedy (New York: Liveright, 1994), p. 167.

2   I am thinking of my colleagues in the Master of Arts in Applied Healing Arts program at Tai Sophia Institute in Laurel, Maryland. See http://www.tai.edu.

3   I think here of distinctions used in the EST training of Werner Erhard with its reliance on some of the work of Fernando Flores.

4   See Shunryu Suzuki, *Zen Mind, Beginner's Mind* (New York & Tokyo: Weatherhill, 1970), p. 21.

5   "Sheikh Muzaffer [a modern spiritual teacher in the Sufi Halveti-Jerrahi order] used to say that every smile and every kind word softens the heart, but every hurtful word or action hardens it." See Robert Frager, *Heart, Self and Soul: The Sufi Psychology of Growth, Balance and Harmony* (Wheaton, IL: Quest Books, 1999), p. 62.

6   See Dante, *Divine Comedy*, Purgatorio, Canto IX.

7   See Coleman Barks, trans. *The Soul of Rumi: A New Collection of Ecstatic Poems* (San Francisco: HarperSanFrancisco, 2001), p. 225.

8   "How Do You Keep the Music Playing?" Music by Michel Legrand, lyrics by Marilyn and Alan Bergman (WB Music-ASCAP).

9   For more on this key distinction, see my book *Living Large: Transformative Work at the Intersection of Ethics and Spirituality* (Laurel, MD: Tai Sophia Institute, 2004), especially the first three chapters.

10   The Ever-Present Origin is a phrase from Jean Gebser. See his *The Ever-Present Origin*, trans. Noel Barstad with Algis Mickunas (Athens, OH: Ohio University Press, 1985). The still point is an image from T. S. Eliot's "Four Quartets." See T. S. Eliot, *The Complete Poems and Plays: 1909–1950* (New York: Harcourt, Brace and Company, 1952), "The Four Quartets, Burnt Norton," p. 119. The phrase "the love that moves the sun and the other stars" comes from the last lines of Dante's *Divine Comedy*.

11   I refer to what is called in Islam "The Day of Alast," referring to a covenant between God and humankind prior to creation. "Am I not [a-lastu] your Lord [bi-rabbi-kum]?" They [the humans] said, "Yes, we do testify." However paradoxically expressed, this is a way to affirm who we are in the widest possible context. See Qu'ran 7:172.

12   See Genesis 1:26–27.

13   David Brazier (Dharmavidya), a teacher in the Amida or Pure Land strand of Buddhism, translates the Japanese word "bombu" as "a foolish being of wayward passion." See David Brazier (Dharmavidya), *Who Loves Dies Well: On the Brink of Buddha's Pure Land* (Winchester, UK: O Books Division of John Hunt Publishing Ltd, 2007) p. 12.

14   Lyrics copyright 1973 Ram's Horn Music. See http://www.bobdylan.com/#/songs/foreveryoung.

Chapter 2

1   See Thich Nhat Hanh, *Present Moment, Wonderful Moment: Mindfulness Verses for Daily Living* (Berkley, CA: Parallax Press, 2006), p. 7.

2   Part of what is called the West Wall Inscription. It is from the office of Chang Tsai, an eleventh-century administrator in China.

3   The phrase "the feeling intellect" I take from Wordsworth; the phrase "the educated heart" I take from Robert Bly.

4   See Dante's *Divine Comedy*, the Paradiso, Canto 30, lines 40–42 describing the Empyrean. The lines are especially beautiful in the original: *luce intellectual, piena d'amore; amor di vero ben, pien di letizia; letizia che trascende ogne dolore.*

5   See Coleman Barks, *Delicious Laughter: Rambunctious Teaching Stories from the Mathnawi* (Athens, GA: Maypop Books, 1990), pp. 25–26.

6   Historian and social critic, Ivan Illich, speaks of this in his *In the Vineyard of the Text* (Chicago: University of Chicago Press, 1993). The book, as a commentary on Hugh of St. Victor's Didascalicon, traces the culture of reading and the book from the twelfth century to the present.

7   In another sense, the student never stops learning — yet perhaps dies to one sort of learning to be reborn into another.

8   I came across the term "kindom" in reading colleague Rebecca Todd Peters' book *In Search of the Good Life: The Ethics of Globalization* (New York: Continuum, 2004). Professor Peters writes: "I embrace Ada Maria Isasi-Diaz's transformation of the concept of 'kingdom' and its patriarchal, hierarchal connotations to the concept of 'kindom,' which represents the 'kinship' of all creation and the promise of a just future. See Ada Maria Isasi-Diaz, *Mujerista Theology: A Theology for the Twenty-first Century* (Maryknoll, NY: Orbis Books, 1996), 103 n8." The comments occur in the Peters' book on p. 33, endnote 16 to chapter 2.

9   The song takes up a prayer by St. Richard of Chichester who prayed on his deathbed: "Thanks be to Thee, my Lord Jesus Christ. For all the benefits Thou hast given me. For all the pains and insults Thou hast borne for me. O most merciful Redeemer, friend and brother. May I know Thee more clearly, Love Thee more dearly, Follow Thee more nearly."

10   Roger Walsh, *Essential Spirituality* (New York: John Wiley & Sons, Inc., 1999), pp. 60–61.

11   I am echoing here a song of the Community of Thich Nhat Hanh, which I learned at a retreat with Thây at Stonehill College in Easton, MA, August 12–17, 2007:

> "Happiness is here and now. I have dropped my worries. Nowhere to go, nothing to do. No longer in a hurry."

And the second stanza:

> "Happiness is here and now. I have dropped my worries. Somewhere to go, something to do. But I don't need to hurry."

12   The core story can be found in Martin Buber, *Tales of the Hasidim: Later Masters* (New York: Schocken Books, 1948; 1974), pp. 249-250. Buber refers to him as Simha Bunam of Pzhysha.

13   Galatians 2:20.

14   The story appears in all three of the synoptic gospels. See Mark 10:17–22, Matthew 19:16–22, and Luke 18:18–23.

15   See Mohammad Ali Jamnia and Mojdeh Bayat, *Under the Sufi's Cloak: Stories of Abu Sa'id and His Mystical Teachings* (Beltsville, MD: Writers' Inc. International, 1995), p. 95.

16   See Eckhart Tolle, *The Power of Now* (Novato, CA: New World Library, 1999), p. 187.

17   I first came across this word play "nowhere and now here" through my mentor Frederick Franck. See Frederick Franck, *Pilgrimage to Now / Here* (Maryland, NY: Orbis Books, 1974). This work becomes part of a larger work in Frederick Franck, *Fingers Pointing toward the Sacred: A Twentieth Century Pilgrimage on the Eastern and Western Way* (Junction City, OR: Beacon Point Press, 1994).

18   The three poisons of Buddhism appear as the second of the Four Noble Truths, after the first truth that there is suffering. I would distinguish necessary and unnecessary suffering. The three poisons are, in my way of phrasing things, the causes of unnecessary suffering. As we diminish them, we diminish unnecessary suffering. This is the third noble truth. The Eight-fold Path – the fourth noble truth – is the set of practices that keep us on the way of well-being. For more on these themes, see my book *Living Large: Transformative Work at the Intersection of Ethics and Spirituality* (Laurel, MD: Tai Sophia Institute, 2004), especially chapter 11.

Chapter 3

1   See Dylan Thomas, "Poem in October" in *The Collected Poems of Dylan Thomas: 1934–1952* (New York: New Directions Books, 1957), p. 113.

2   The challenge to those reared in a culture of doing is to stop seeing the tasks of Autumn as more striving — striving to let go! This confuses repression with releasement. The beliefs and roles that bind us are illusory to begin with. They never were the truth of things. Letting them go is waking up to that!

3   See Wendell Berry, *Collected Poems: 1957–1982* (San Francisco: North Point Press, 1985), p. 69.

4   For more on Ryōkan, see John Stevens, trans. *Dewdrops on a Lotus Leaf: Zen Poems of Ryokan* (Boston: Shambhala, 1996).

5   Thich Nhat Hanh, *Peace Is Every Step: The Path of Mindfulness in Everyday Life* (New York: Bantam Books, 1992), p. 95.

6   Thomas Berry (1914–2009) was a Roman Catholic priest of the Passionist order who recontextualized religion, education, commerce, and government in a cosmological or cosmic context. See his *The Great Work* (New York: Bell Tower, 1999), p. 16 and elsewhere, for the distinction between viewing the natural world as a collection of objects vs. viewing the natural world as a communion of subjects. See also his *The Dream of the Universe* (San Francisco: Sierra Club Books, 1988) and, with Brian Swimme, *The Universe Story* (San Francisco: HarperSanFrancisco, 1992).

7   See footnote 5, chapter 1. I believe that this quote is from the Sufi teacher, Sheikh Muzaffer. "Sheikh Muzaffer used to say that every smile and every kind word softens the heart but every hurtful word or action hardens it." See Robert Frager, *Heart, Self and Soul* (Wheaton, IL: Quest Books, 1999), p. 62.

8   These Four Immeasurable Abodes (or Minds) — also known as the Brahma Viharas — are love or loving-kindness (maître), compassion (karuna), joy or sympathetic joy (mudita), and equanimity (upeksha). I am following the treatment of Thich Nhat Hanh here. See Thich Nhat Hanh, *The Heart of the Buddha's Teaching* (New York:

Broadway Books, 1992), pp. 169–175, as well as Thich Nhat Hanh, *Teachings on Love* (Berkeley, CA: Parallax Press, 1998), pp. 1–9. See also Jack Kornfield, *A Path with a Heart* (New York: Bantam Books, 1993), pp. 190–191, where he notes that the near enemy of love is attachment; the near enemy of compassion is pity; the near enemy of sympathetic joy is comparison; and the near enemy of equanimity is indifference.

9   See the thirteenth-fourteenth-century German mystic, Meister Eckhart's short treatise *On Detachment* (Middle High German *abegescheidenheit* — releasement or letting go) in Edmund Colledge and Bernard McGinn, editors and translators, *Meister Eckhart: The Essential Sermons, Commentaries, Treatises and Defense* (Mawah, NJ: Paulist Press, 1981), pp. 285–294. The "hinge" metaphor is on page 291. On Eckhart, see also Reiner Schürmann, *Wandering Joy: Meister Eckhart's Mystical Philosophy* (Great Barrington, MA: Lindisfarne Books, 2001).

10   See Coleman Barks with John Moyne, A. J. Arberry, Reynold Nicholson, *The Essential Rumi* (San Francisco: HarperSanFrancisco, 1995), p. 109.

11   As the Upanishads teach: Tat tvam asi [the One, the Ultimate] — thou art that.

12   See T. E. Lawrence, *Seven Pillars of Wisdom* (Harmondsworth, England: Penguin and Jonathan Cape, 1971), p. 364. The quote is a favorite of the Notre Dame theologian and spiritual writer John S. Dunne.

13   Quoted in Nancy Wilson Ross, *The World of Zen* (New York: Random House Vintage Books, 1960), p. 271. See also Frederick Franck, *Echoes from the Bottomless Well* (New York: Random House Vintage Books, 1985), p. 91.

Chapter 4

1   The translation is by Robert Bly, see Robert Bly, ed. *The Soul is Here for Its Own Joy* (Hopewell, NJ: Ecco Press, 1995), p. 246.

2   See Genesis 1:1–2.

3   See *The Essential Rumi*, trans. Coleman Barks with John Moyne (San Francisco: HarperSanFranciso, 1995), p. 12.

4   The young philosopher was Anne Joy Cahill-Swenson, daughter of Ann Cahill and Neil Swenson. The incident took place in July 2008 when Anne Joy was almost 5 years old.

5   Paul Eluard quoted in John Tarrant, *The Light Inside the Dark* (San Francisco: HarperSanFrancisco, 1998), p. 4.

6   I owe the phrase "ruthless certainties" to my friend Robert Knowles. It echoes a theme that the cultural critic Ivan Illich sounded throughout his writings.

7   See William Blake's poem "The Marriage of Heaven and Hell."

8   I take the term "severe teachers" from Reb Zalman. See Zalman Schachter-Shalomi and Ronald S. Miller, *From Age-ing to Sage-ing* (New York: Warner Books, 1995), Exercise 7: "A Testimonial Dinner for the Severe Teachers," pp. 279–280.

9   Some experience an opening of the sense of sight, others, a subtle hearing. Perhaps all the senses can be activated in new and different ways.

10   The lines are the closing lines of T. S. Eliot's "Four Quartets."

11   For more on Byron Katie and the turn around, see Byron Katie with Stephen Mitchell, *Loving What Is: Four Questions That Can Change Your Life* (New York: Three Rivers Press, 2002).

12   For more on Winter and the Fool, see my *Living Large: Transformative Work at the Intersection of Ethics and Spirituality* (Laurel, MD: Tai Sophia Institute, 2004), chapter 12.

13   See Zalman Schachter-Shalomi and Ronald S. Miller, *From Age-ing to Sage-ing* (New York: Warner Books, 1995), pp. 271–272.

14   Buckminster Fuller's remarks can be found in the February 1972 issue of *Playboy* magazine.

15   I am thinking here of Judaism, Christianity, and Islam, which all accept and respect the Hebrew scriptures — what Christians call the Old Testament.

16   I am echoing here St. Nicholas of Cusa's remark: "In all faces is shown the Face of Faces, veiled and as if in a riddle . . ." Quoted in Frederick Franck, *The Zen of Seeing* (New York: Random House Vintage Books, 1973), p. 81.

17   See Dante, *Divine Comedy*, Paradiso, Canto III, lines 85–87.

18   See *The Tao Te Ching*, trans. Gia-Fu Feng and Jane English (New York: Random House Vintage Books, 1972), chapter 15. Passage modified for inclusive language.

19   The translation is by Robert Bly. See Robert Bly, ed., *The Soul is Here for Its Own Joy* (Hopewell, NJ: Ecco Press, 1995), p. 246.

Afterword

1   See footnote 11, chapter 2. Many of the chants are published. See *Plum Village Chanting and Recitation Book*, compiled by Thich Nhat Hanh and the Monks and Nuns of Plum Village (Berkeley, CA: Parallax Press, 2000). However, this "Happiness is here and now" song I learned at a retreat with Thây at Stonehill College in Easton Massachusetts, August 12–17, 2007.

2   See footnote 2, Introduction.

3   In Eastern thought, especially Taoism, the upward and outward side of the circle is the *yang* side and the downward and inward side is the *yin* side. Of course, as the familiar symbol shows, nothing is completely yang or completely yin, for in the yin is a dot of yang and in the yang, a dot of yin. Yin originally referred to the shady side of the mountain and yang to the sunny side of the mountain. Same mountain, now shady and later sunny; now sunny and later shady. In a 24-hour period, on the yin side there is night and on the yang side, day. In a year, spring and summer manifest yang; autumn and winter manifest yin. Also we might think of the yang side as doing, giving, speaking, and the yin side as being, receiving, listening. The approach to the seasons I dwell in encompasses all of this.

4   When we picture the circle vertically we see rising and falling energy. The side of service companioned by the side of stillness or deepening. When we draw the circle horizontally, we think of breathing in and then breathing out — inner/outer rather than up/down. Breathing out, we serve; breathing in, we deepen. Stillness or deepening is for the sake of service; service is for the sake of deepening all our kin. A virtuous rather than vicious circle.

5　I am drawing on the Buddhist Eight-fold Path here, a path meant to diminish our clinging, condemning, and identifying and thus increase our love, compassion, and wisdom. The Eight-fold Path can be seen as a circle or spiral. Each turn begins with (1) insight and (2) resolve (which turn out at deeper levels to be the great wisdom that is also the great compassion). Gaining a measure of insight and compassionate response, one again embarks on the Conduct Segment of the path (upward and outward): (3) speaking, (4) acting, (5) right vocation. Then there is a turning into the downward and inward side, the Meditative Segment: (6) steady, (7) mindful, (8) concentration. And the result is again (1) greater insight and (2) greater resolve. And round again. My chant is: Knowing, Loving, here we go now. Speaking, Acting, Right vocation. Steady, Mindful, Concentration. Knowing, Loving, here we go now. (Beat out the time, one beat for each syllable!)

6　For more detail on this lake analogy, see my book *Living Large: Transformative Work at the Intersection of Ethics and Spirituality* (Laurel, MD: Tai Sophia Press, 2004), pp. 58–62.

7　As Socrates would say, you and I (at this stage) are doubly ignorant. We do not know what is real (ignorance #1) and we do not know we do not know (ignorance #2)!

8　See, for example, Arthur J. Deikman, *The Observing Self: Mysticism and Psychotherapy* (Boston: Beacon Press, 1982).

9　For more on these matters, see Chalmers Brothers, *Language and the Pursuit of Happiness* (Naples, FL: New Possibilities Press, 2005).

10　Of course, it is possible to go back rather than forward — to redo the first half of life in the second half. As musicians say, to take it from the top. Da capo. Get a new love. Start a new career. I think I understand the impulse. Encore careers have their place. Yet I am convinced that the later years have their own gifts, their own insights, their own ways to work and to love. For me, Forest Dweller and Sage hold the clues.

11　This is a quote from an interview given to Knud Rasmussen, the Danish anthropologist and ethnographer of the Inuit peoples. See Robert Bly, *News of the Universe: Poems of Twofold Consciousness* (San Francisco: Sierra Club Books, 1980), p. 257.

12　A powerful way of releasing is what Byron Katie calls "The Work." See Byron Katie

with Stephen Mitchell, *Loving What Is: Four Questions That Can Change Your Life* (New York: Random House Harmony Books, 2002), and their volume *A Thousand Names for Joy: Living in Harmony with the Way Things Are* (New York: Random House Harmony Books, 2007) as well as *Who Would You Be Without Your Story? Dialogues with Byron Katie*, ed. Carol Williams (New York: Hay House, 2008).

13   For more on practices of Autumn, see my book *Living Large: Transformative Work at the Intersection of Ethics and Spirituality*, chapter 11, pp. 167–184.

14   For more on practices of Winter, see my book *Living Large: Transformative Work at the Intersection of Ethics and Spirituality*, chapter 12, pp. 185–199.

15   This is a saying of the prophet Muhammad. Where the original has remembrance of God (Allah), I have used "the One," so as to echo the theme of oneness in all of the religions of the book and beyond. For the quote, see Kabir Edmund Helminski, *Living Presence: A Sufi Way to Mindfulness and the Essential Self* (New York: Jeremy P. Tacher/Perigee Books, 1992), p. 67.